This book belongs to:

____

Copyright © 2025 by Tughra Books
24 23 22 21 1 2 3 4

All rights reserved. No part of this book may be reproduced or transmitted in any form or by any means, electronic or mechanical, including photocopying, recording or by any information storage and retrieval system without permission in writing from the Publisher.

Published by Tughra Books
335 Clifton Ave.
Clifton, NJ, 07011, USA
www.tughrabooks.com

ISBN: 979-8-89729-510-4

Mini Muslims Series ISBN 9781597849692

WHO ARE the Prophets?

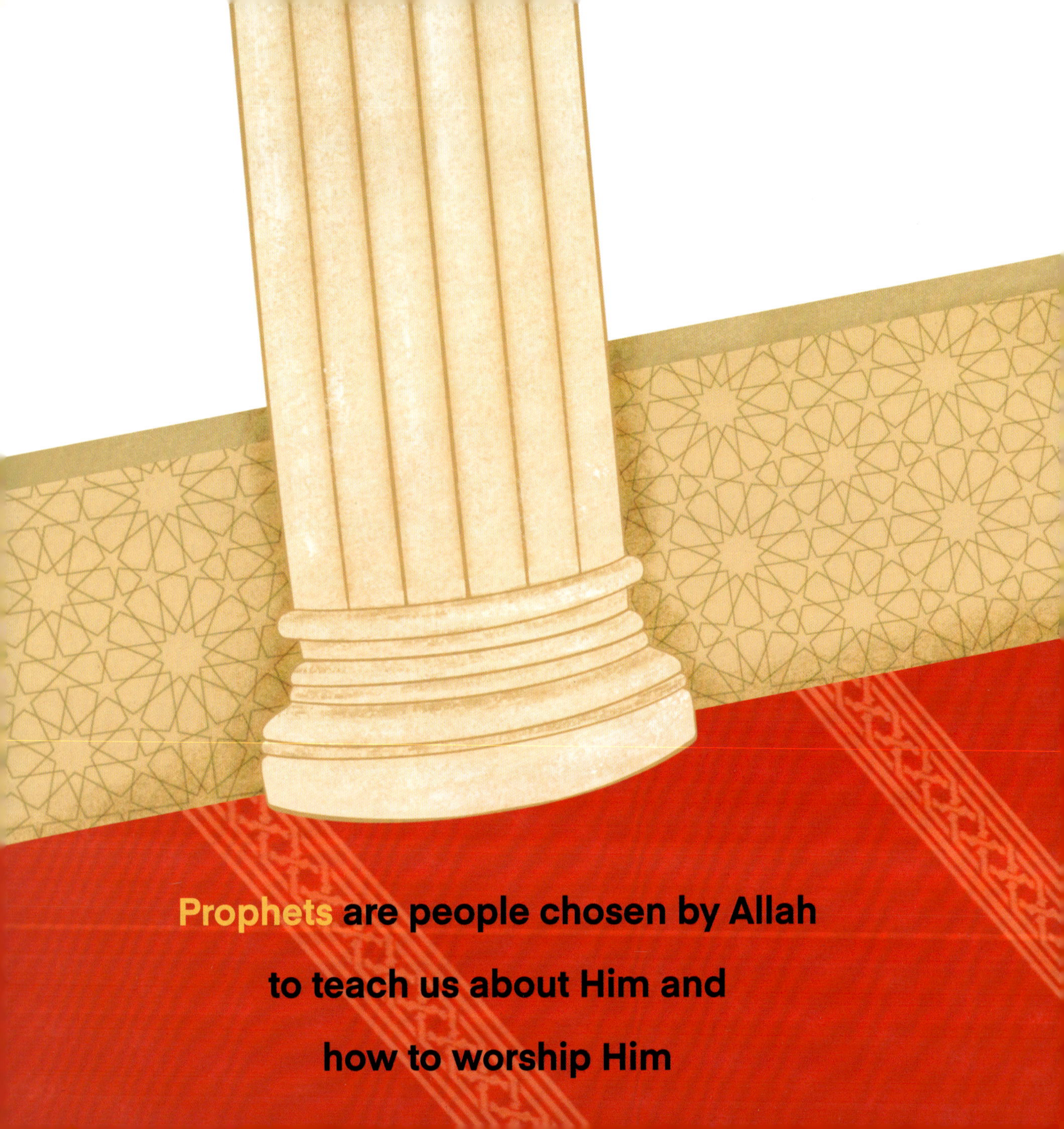

Prophets are people chosen by Allah
to teach us about Him and
how to worship Him

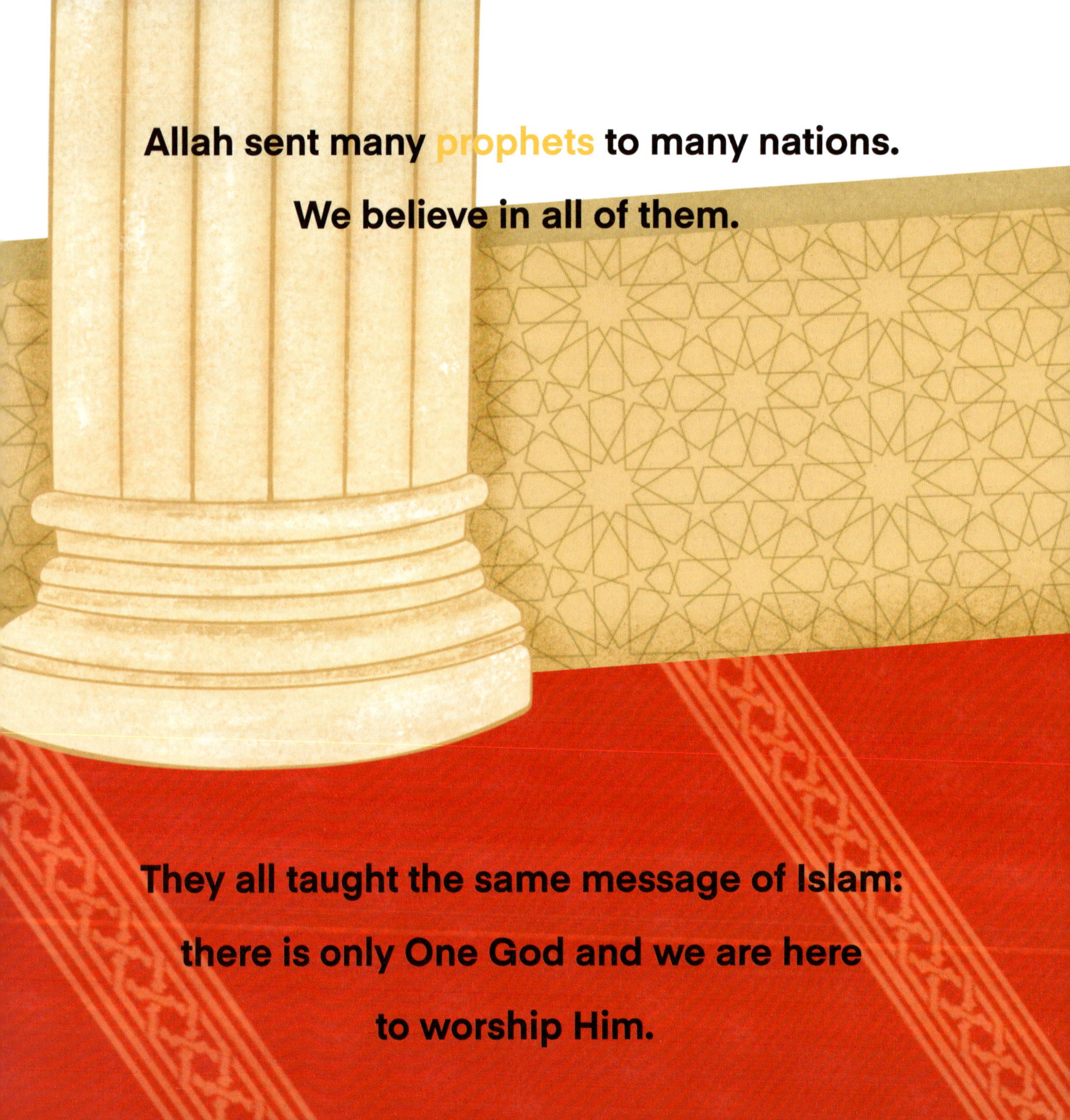

Allah sent many prophets to many nations.

We believe in all of them.

They all taught the same message of Islam: there is only One God and we are here to worship Him.

Adam
Nuh
Ibrahim

are the names of some of the prophets.

Muhammad (pbuh)

is the last and final prophet that Allah sent.

We love all

the prophets!